THE POWER OF IMAGINATION

"…… and this they begin to do: and now nothing will be restrained from them, which they have imagined to do."

Genesis 11:6

By
Franklin N. Abazie

The Power of Imagination

COPYRIGHT 2018 BY Franklin N Abazie
ISBN: 978-1-945-133-87-9
All right reserved. This book or any portion thereof may not be reproduced or used in any manner whatsoever without the express written permission of the publisher, except for the use of brief quotations in a book review. All Bible quotes are from King James Version and others as noted.

Published by: F N ABAZIE PUBLISHING HOUSE---
a.k.a,
Empowerment Bookstore:

That I may publish with the voice of thanksgiving and tell of all thy wondrous works. **Psalms26:7**

To order additional copies, wholesales or booking: Call the Church office (973-372-7518)
or Empowerment Bookstore Hotline 973-393-8518
Worship address:
343 Sanford Avenue Newark New Jersey 07106
Administrative Head Office address:
33 Schley Street Newark New Jersey 07112
Email:pastorfranknto@yahoo.com
Website www.fnabaziehealingministries.org
Publishing House: www.fnabaziepublishinghouse.org

This book is a production of F N Abazie Publishing House.

A publication Arms of Miracle of God Ministries 2018
First Edition

CONTENTS

THE MANDATE OF THE COMMISSION............iv

ARMS OF THE COMMISSION............................v

INTRODUCTION..viii

CHAPTER 1

1. What is the Power of Imagination? 42

CHAPTER 2

2. The Power of Vision..54

CHAPTER 3

3. Prayer of Salvation..83

CHAPTER 4

4. About the Author...91

THE MANDATE OF THE COMMISSION

"THE MOMENT IS DUE TO IMPACT YOUR WORLD THROUGH THE REVIVAL OF THE HEALING & MIRACLE MINISTRY OF JESUS CHRIST OF NAZARETH.

I AM SENDING YOU TO RESTORE HEALTH UNTO THEE AND I WILL HEAL THEE OF THY WOUNDS, SAID THE LORD OF HOST."

ARMS OF THE COMMISSION

1) F N Abazie Ministries-Miracle of God Ministries (Miracle Chapel Intl)

2) F N Abazie TV Ministries: Global Television Ministry Outreach.

3) F N Abazie Radio Ministries: Radio Broadcasting Outreach.

4) F N Abazie Publishing House: Book Publication.

5) F N Abazie Bible School: also called Word of Healing Bible School (W.O.H.B.S)

6) F N Abazie Evangelistic Ass: Miracle of God Ministries: Global Crusade

7) Empowerment Bookstore: Book distribution.

8) F N Abazie Helping Hands: Meeting the help of the needy world wide

9) F N Abazie Disaster Recovery Mission: Global Disaster Recovery.

10) F N Abazie Prison Ministry: Prison Ministry for all convicts "Second chance"

Some of our ministry arms are waiting the appointed time to commence

FAVOR CONFESSION

Father thank you for making me righteous and accepted through the blood of Jesus Christ. Because of that, I am blessed and highly favored by God. I am the subject of your affection. Your favor surrounds me as a shield, and the first thing that people see around me is your favored shield.

Thank you that I have favor with you and man today. All day long people go out of their way to bless me and help me. I have favor with everyone that I deal with today. Doors that were once closed are now opened for me. I receive preferential treatment, and I have special privileges, I am Gods favored child.

No good thing will he withhold from me. Because of Gods favor my enemies cannot triumph over my life. I have supernatural increase and promotion. I declare restoration to everything that the devil has stolen from my life. I have honor in the midst of my adversaries and an increase in assets, especially in real estate and expansion of

Because I am highly favored by God, I experience great victories, supernatural turnarounds, and miraculous breakthrough in the midst of great impossibilities. I receive recognition, prominence, and honor. Petitions are granted to me even by ungodly authorities. Policies, rules, regulations, and laws are changed and reverse on my behalf.

I win battles that I don't even have to fight, because God fights them for me. This is the day, the set time and the designated moment for me to experience the free favor of God, that profusely and lavishly abound on my behalf in Jesus name. Amen.

INTRODUCTION

"And the Lord said, Behold, the people is one, and they have all one language; and this they begin to do: and now nothing will be restrained from them, which they have imagined to do." **Genesis11:6**

The power of Imagination literally means our ability to form a mental picture of our actual future. In this context, it is our ability to capture our future through the pages of the scripture.

Albert Einstein once said *"Imagination is more important than knowledge. For knowledge is limited to all we now know and understand, while imagination embraces the entire world, and all there ever will be to know and understand."*

Unless we can see our future through the eyes of our imagination, we will not be able to rule the world. Remember, Napoleon Bonaparte once said *"Imagination rules the world."*

In this small book I have shared a few revelations that will help anyone achieve a great future. Again, Napoleon Bonaparte once said *"Ability is nothing without opportunity."* I encourage you to put away all your secular knowledge and enjoy this book as inspired by the Holy Spirit of the Living God.

This book is not a book of logic, but a book of wisdom. A great man once said *"logic will get you from point A to point Z, but imagination will take you everywhere."*

As you read this small book, imagine your future in a mental picture. I encourage you to pursue it with every energy in you. By this time you should able to have formed a mental picture of your desired future. Go for it!

Happy Reading!

HIS DESTINY WAS THE CROSS….

HIS PURPOSE WAS LOVE…..

HIS REASON WAS YOU….

"And the Lord said, Behold, the people is one, and they have all one language; and this they begin to do: and now nothing will be restrained from them, which they have imagined to do."

Genesis11:6

"Casting down imaginations, and every high thing that exalteth itself against the knowledge of God, and bringing into captivity every thought to the obedience of Christ."

2cor10:3

Prayer Points

"If ye shall ask any thing in my name, I will do it.." **John 14:14**

Holy Spirit of God frustrate and disappoint, every one that is against my life and family, in the name of Jesus.

Father Lord destroy every demonic networks and traps against my progress in life in the name of Jesus.

Fire of God, destroy every demonic projection and curses against my life and destiny in the name of Jesus.

Every spell and curses pronounced against my destiny, break, in the name of Jesus.

Hand of God cage every power militating against my rising in life, in the name of Jesus.

Power of God silent every voice raising a counter motion against my elevation, in the mighty name of Jesus.

Blood of Jesus neutralize every spirit of Balaam hired to hinder my life, ministry, and career, the name of Jesus.

Fire of God destroy every curse that I have brought into my life through ignorance and disobedience, break by fire, in the name of Jesus.

Ancient of day destroy every power harassing my ministry in the name of Jesus.

Father God deliver me from invincible forces militating against my life and destiny.

Power of God frustrate every coven and demonic network, designed to frustrate and hinder my success in life, in the name of Jesus.

I dismantle every strong hold designed to imprison my talent in the mighty name of Jesus.

I reject every cycle of frustration, in the name of Jesus.

Power of God paralyze every agent assigned to frustrate my life in the name of Jesus.

Finger of God, grant me supernatural speed against all my contenders in the name of Jesus.

By the blood of Jesus, I destroy every familiar spirit caging my life and career.

Fire of God arrest every demonic agents, assigned to police my destiny and marriage.

By the blood of Jesus, I proclaim no weapon fashioned against me shall ever prosper.

Holy Spirit of God break me through and forward in life in the mighty name of Jesus.

God, smash me and renew my strength, in the name of Jesus.

Holy Spirit, open my eyes to see beyond the visible to the invisible, in the name of Jesus.

Father Lord grant me strength and power in the name of Jesus.

O Lord, liberate my spirit to follow the leading of the Holy Spirit.

Holy Spirit, teach me to pray through problems instead of praying about, it in the name of Jesus.

Father Lord, deliver me from the false accusation in life, in the name of Jesus.

By the blood of Jesus, every evil spiritual padlock and evil chain hindering my success, be roasted, in the name of Jesus.

By the blood of Jesus I rebuke every spirit of spiritual deafness and blindness in my life, in the name of Jesus.

Father Lord, empower me to dominate the enemy of my destiny in the name of Jesus.

Jesus Christ of Nazareth, heal my infirmities in the name of Jesus.

Lord, anoint my eyes and my ears that they may see and hear wondrous things from heaven.

Father Lord, anoint me with power and authority to dominate all my enemies in the name of Jesus.

Fire of God roast every giant rising up against my life and career.

Holy Spirit of God destroy all my oppressors in the name of Jesus.

Angels of good new, bring my good news to me in the mighty name of Jesus.

Every strong man holding me down, lose your hold now in the name of Jesus.

I nullify every demonic prediction over my life in the name of Jesus.

By the blood of Jesus, I flush out every polluted deposit of the enemy in my life.

By the blood of Jesus, I paralyze every enemy of my promotion in the name of Jesus.

Father Lord, destroy any power tormenting my life that is not from you.

Holy Ghost fire, ignite the fire of revival in my life.

By the blood of Jesus, I declare victory over every conflicting trial.

By the Blood of Jesus, I command the arrest of every demonic spirit, militating against my life .

By the blood of Jesus, I proclaimed the blood of Jesus, over every device of the enemy.

By the blood of Jesus, I revoke stagnation and hardship over my life in the name of Jesus.

Holy Ghost fire, destroy every satanic arrangement in my life, in the name of Jesus.

It is written, *"do not be afraid of sudden terror; nor of the trouble from the wicked when it comes; for the Lord will be your confidence. And will keep your foot from being caught."* **(Proverb 3:26)**.

Therefore, O Lord, cover us and our loved ones from the activities of terrorists, in Jesus name!

It is written, *"avenge me of my adversary"* **(Luke. 18:3)**.

Therefore, O Lord, arise and avenge us of all my adversaries in the name of Jesus!

It is written, *"they fought from the heavens; the stars from their courses fought against Sisera."* **(Judges. 5:20)**.

Therefore O heavens, fight for us in Jesus name!

It is written, *"I will purge the rebels from among you, and those who transgress against me; I will bring them out of the country where they dwell, but they shall not enter the land of Israel. They will know that I am the Lord."* **(Ezekiel. 20:38)**

Therefore, O Lord, purge and sanitize our household in the name of Jesus!

It is written, *"then it was so, after all your wickedness – "woe, woe to you!" says the Lord God."* **(Ezekiel. 16:23)**

Therefore, woe unto all the vessels that the enemy is using to do us harm in the name of Jesus!

It is written, *"behold therefore, I stretch out my hand against you, admonished your allotment, and gave you up to the will of those who hate you..."* **(Ezekiel. 16:27)**

Therefore, let our enemies be delivered into the hands of their enemies in Jesus name!

It is written, *"you shall be for fuel of fire; your blood shall be in the midst of the land. You shall not be remembered, for I the Lord have spoken."* **(Ezekiel. 21:32)**

Therefore, let all our spiritual enemies become fuel for divine fire in Jesus name!

It is written, *"Then they will know that I am the Lord, when I have set a fire in Egypt and all her helpers are destroyed."* **(Ezekiel. 30:8).**

Therefore, O Lord, let all the helpers of our enemies be destroyed in the name of Jesus.

It is written, *"and the people to whom they prophesy shall be cast out in the streets of Jerusalem because of the famine and the sword; they will have no one to bury them – them nor their wives, their sons nor their daughters – for I will pour their wickedness on them."* **(Jer. 14:16).**

Therefore, O Lord, pour the wickedness of those who seek to destroy us upon their own heads in the name of Jesus!

It is written, *"Call together the archers against Babylon. All you who bend the bow encamp against it all around; let none of them escape. Repay her according to her work; According to all she has done, do to her; for she has been poured against the Lord, against the Holy one of Israel."* **(Jer. 50:29).**

Therefore, let all the hosts of the Lord turn against our spiritual enemies in Jesus name!

It is written, *"let God arise, let His enemies be scattered; let those also who hate him flee before him."* **(Psalms. 68:1)**.

Therefore, O God, arise and let all your enemies in our lives be scattered in Jesus name!

It is written, *"and He that searches the hearts knows what the mind of the spirit is, because He makes intercession for the saints according to the will of God."* **(Romans 8:27)**

Therefore, the intercessory prayers of Jesus, who is seated on the right hand of the throne of God, will not be in vain over our lives, in the name of Jesus.

It is written, *"The Lord is your keeper; the Lord is the shade at your right hand. The sun shall not strike you by day, nor the moon by night. The Lord shall preserve you from all evil; He shall preserve your soul. The Lord shall preserve our going out and our coming in from this time forth, and even forevermore."* **(Psalms. 121:5-8)**

Therefore, O Lord, spread your covering of fire and the blood of Jesus over us and our loved ones, in the name of Jesus.

It is written, *"Rejoice always, pray without ceasing, in everything give thanks; for this is the will of God in Christ Jesus for you."* **(1 Thess. 5:16:18)**.

Therefore, we thank you Father, for raising a spiritual shield over our loved ones and us. Thank you for giving us the heart for appreciating everything you are doing for us. Thank you for filling our hearts and our home with joy and peace that surpasses all understanding. Blessed be your name for all the answers to our prayers in the name of Jesus!

You are holy, holy, Lord God Almighty, who was and is and is to come, Amen!

O Lord, let our season of divine intervention appear in the name of Jesus!

O you gates in the heavenlies standing against our destiny, lift up your heads in the name of Jesus!

O you gates in the waters standing against our destiny, lift up your heads in the name of Jesus!

O you gates in the earth standing against our destiny, lift up your heads in the name of Jesus!

O you gates under the earth standing against our destiny, lift up your heads in the name of Jesus!

O God, arise and destroy every gate keeper assigned against our lives in the name of Jesus!

We break the backbone of every spirit of scarcity in our lives in the name of Jesus!

O Lord anoint our eyes to see divine opportunities in the name of Jesus!

Lord let every blindness to the treasures of our lives be cleared in the name of Jesus!

Let our divine helpers appear in the name of Jesus!

We declare, O Lord, that the rest of our lives will be better than the first part, in Jesus name!

We declare, O Lord that will overcome obstacles and defeat every enemy, in Jesus name!

We declare, O Lord that every blessing and promise that you put in our hearts will come to pass because this is our time for favor, in Jesus name!

We declare, O Lord that this is a new season of increase in our lives. We speak health, wisdom, creativity, divine connections, and supernatural opportunities. They are coming our way, in Jesus name!

We declare, O Lord that we choose faith over fear. We are victorious in faith, in Jesus name!

We declare, O Lord that that we are not just surviving, this is our time to thrive in prosperity, in Jesus name!

We declare, O Lord that we will believe that we have received in the spirit even though we do not see anything happening in the flesh, in Jesus name!

We declare, O Lord that our rewards are being transferred to us because we remain in faith, in Jesus name!

We declare, O Lord that doubt will not ruin our optimistic spirit, in Jesus name!

We declare, O Lord that we are prisoners of hope and get up every morning expecting your favor, in Jesus name!

We declare, O Lord that you will do amazing things in our lives, in Jesus name!

We declare, O Lord that we are closer to your abundant blessing than we think, our time has come, your promises will come to pass, in Jesus name!

We declare, O Lord that we will stay in an attitude of faith and expectation, in Jesus name!

We declare, O Lord that we are not worried, we know that you are our vindicator. It may seem to be taking a long time, but we will reap in due season if trust in you Lord, in Jesus name!

We declare, O Lord that you know the secret petitions our heart and we believe that they will come to fulfilment, in Jesus name!

We declare, O Lord that you will open new doors for us, in Jesus name!

We declare, O Lord that we will see your goodness, in Jesus name!

We declare, O Lord that this is our time to believe because favor is coming our way, in Jesus name!

We declare, O Lord that you have paved the way to abundant prosperity for us, prosperity more than we can every dream of or imagine, for your sake, in Jesus name!

We declare, O Lord that in your eyes our future is extremely bright, in Jesus name!

We declare, O Lord that we will rise higher and higher and see more of your favor and blessings and we will live the prosperous life you have in store for us, in Jesus name!

We declare, O Lord that we may have a lot of troubles, but we know that everything is going to be alright, in Jesus name!

We declare, O Lord that we have faith because we have put you first, in Jesus name!

We thank you, O Lord that our set time for favor is here, in Jesus name!

We declare, O Lord that our hour of deliverance has come, in Jesus name!

We declare, O Lord that there is no limit to what we can do, in Jesus name!

We declare, O Lord that there is no obstacle we cannot overcome, in Jesus name!

We declare, O Lord that that we have seen your accomplishments and they are good, in Jesus name!

We declare, O Lord that there is no challenge that is too great for us because you are with us, in Jesus name!

We declare, O Lord that you always succeed, in Jesus name!

We declare, O Lord that there is no financial difficulty or situation in our lives that is too great for you to resolve, in Jesus name!

We declare, O Lord that you are our Father Jehovah Jireh and that you own everything and you are our provider, in Jesus name!

We declare, O Lord that your promises declare that we are destined to live a victorious life, in Jesus name!

We declare, O Lord that we are your children, in Jesus name!

We declare, O Lord that the seeds of increase, success, and promotion are taking a new root; your favor will spring forth in our lives in a great way; we will see new seasons of blessings and new seasons of your favor. It's our time to have abundant faith, in Jesus name!

O Lord, it is written; according to your faith, it will be done unto you. Ps. 2:8 says *"ask me and I will give you the nations as your inheritance."*

Therefore, we ask you Lord to fulfil our highest hopes and dreams, in Jesus name!

We ask you this day, O Lord to give us our abundant blessing now, in Jesus name!

We dare to exercise our faith by asking you O Lord so that we may receive indeed, in Jesus name!

We thank you O Lord that for encouraging our faith, in Jesus name!

We declare, O Lord that this is our time for favor, in Jesus name!

We declare, O Lord that this is our time to prosper abundantly, in Jesus name!

We declare, O Lord that this is our time to have instant answers to prayer, in Jesus name!

We declare, O Lord that this is our time to ask and receive, in Jesus name!

We declare, O Lord that this is our time to thank you and testify for answered prayer, in Jesus name!

We declare, O Lord that we are blessed and that goodness and mercy are following us right now, in Jesus name!

We declare, O Lord that you favor is surrounding us like a shield – you prosper us even in the desert, in Jesus name!

We declare, O Lord that you have great things for us in the spirit and that you have already released favor into our prayers, in Jesus name!

We declare, O Lord that you are a great and Holy God, in Jesus name!

It is written, *"Delight yourself in the Lord and he will give you the desires of your heart."* **(Ps 37:4)**.

We therefore declare, O Lord that we delight in you because you are our Father God and because we are your children you have made us the head and not the tail. You want to take us to a new level of prosperity, in Jesus name!

We declare, O Lord that because we are your children, we are more than conquerors, in Jesus name!

We declare, O Lord that we are blessed and you supply all our needs. We have more than enough, in Jesus name!

We declare, O Lord that we have abundant favor indeed, in Jesus name!

We declare, O Lord that we are filled indeed with the presence of the Holy Spirit, in Jesus name!

We declare, O Lord that we have abundant faith indeed, in Jesus name!

We declare, O Lord that you have answered our prayers, in Jesus name!

We declare, O Lord that our debts are all paid up, in Jesus name!

We declare, O Lord that we are healthy, in Jesus name!

We declare, O Lord that we have no lack and that we have more than enough, in Jesus name!

We declare, O Lord that we are extremely blessed so much that we can bless your kingdom, in Jesus name!

We declare, O Lord that we are extremely blessed so much that we can bless others, in Jesus name!

We declare, O Lord that we have entered into an anointing of ease, in Jesus name!

We declare, O Lord that for every opportunity we have missed, every chance we've blown, you will turn the clock and bring bigger and better things across our path, in Jesus name!

We declare, O Lord that we will not settle for less than your best, in Jesus name!

Please restore the time that we have lost, O Lord that, in Jesus name!

Restore our victories, O Lord, in Jesus name!

Restore our lost joy, lost peace, lost health, lost insight, lost faith, lost dedication, and desire to please you, we declare, O Lord in Jesus name!

We declare, O Lord that you use what was meant for our harm to our advantage, in Jesus name!

We declare, O Lord that you are a faithful God, in Jesus name!

We declare, O Lord that you will blossom our lives in ways that we can never imagine, in Jesus name!

We know, O Lord that you will bless us abundantly, in Jesus name!

We know, O Lord that you will provide divine connections, in Jesus name!

We declare, O Lord that we are not suffering – we are blessed, in Jesus name!

We declare, O Lord that our difficulties will give way to new growth, new opportunities, and new vision, in Jesus name!

O Lord let us see your blessing bloom in our lives in ways we would never dreamt possible, in Jesus name!

We declare, O Lord that we will stay in faith, so that what was meant to stop us will not be a stumbling block but a stepping stone taking us to a higher level, in Jesus name!

We declare, O Lord that we are not ordinary, but we are children of the most high God, in Jesus name!

We declare, O Lord that we created to rise above problems, in Jesus name!

We declare victory over strife O Lord, in Jesus name!

We declare, O Lord that no weapon formed against us shall prosper, in Jesus name!

We declare, O Lord that we are healthy and that no sickness shall live in us, in Jesus name!

We declare, O Lord that triumph is our birthright, in Jesus name!

We declare, O Lord that our setbacks are simply setups for greater comebacks that will place us to be better than we were before, in Jesus name!

We declare, O Lord that with you all things are possible, in Jesus name!

We declare, O Lord that we are in agreement with you. We know you have supernatural favor in store for us. You have supernatural opportunities, supernatural healing, and supernatural restoration, in Jesus name!

We declare, O Lord that you want to do unusual things in our lives, in Jesus name!

We declare, O Lord that in faith, we have expectation deep in our spirits, in Jesus name!

We declare, O Lord that this will not be a survival year but a supernatural year in which you will abundantly come through for us, in Jesus name!

We believe, O Lord that you have come through for us, in Jesus name!

We declare, O Lord that because we hope in you, we will not be put to shame, in Jesus name!

We declare, O Lord that your word is right and true, you are faithful in all you do, in Jesus name!

We declare, O Lord that you are our refuge and strength, an ever present helper, in Jesus name!

We declare, O Lord that we will cast our cares on you and you will sustain us, you will never let the righteous fall, in Jesus name!

We declare, O Lord that you are the strength of our hearts and our portion forever, in Jesus name!

We declare, O Lord that you are our dwelling, therefore, no harm will befall us, and no disaster will come near our tent, in Jesus name!

We declare, O Lord that you are our refuge and our fortress, in Jesus name!

We declare, O Lord that you will command your angels concerning us to guard us in all our ways, in Jesus name!

We declare, O Lord that even in darkness the light will dawn for us, in Jesus name!

We declare, O Lord that your word is eternal and stands firm in the heavens, in Jesus name!

We declare, O Lord that your faithfulness will continue throughout all generations, in Jesus name!

We declare, O Lord that you will keep us from harm; you will watch over our lives; you will watch over our coming and our going both now and for evermore, in Jesus name! **(Psalms. 121)**

Thank you O Lord for the assurance that you are watching over us even when we sleep, in Jesus name! **(Psalms. 13:5-6)**

We declare, O Lord that you will drive those that do evil away from us and that you will protect us from their influence, in Jesus name! **(Ps. 66:1-4)**

We will shout with joy to you O Lord, we will sing the glory of your name and make your praise glorious. How awesome are your deeds! So great is your power that your enemies cringe before you, in Jesus name!

We declare, O Lord that that we will give you thanks for you answered us, in Jesus name! **(Psalms. 118:21)**

We declare, O Lord that we will praise you with all our hearts; before the gods we will sing your praise. We will bow down towards your Holy temple and will praise your name for your love and your faithfulness, for you have exalted above all things, your name, and your word, in Jesus name! **(Psalms. 138:1-3)**

"Finally, brethren, whatsoever things are true, whatsoever things are honest, whatsoever things are just, whatsoever things are pure, whatsoever things are lovely, whatsoever things are of good report; if there be any virtue, and if there be any praise, think on these things."

Phil4:8

CHAPTER 1
What is the Power of Imagination?

"And the Lord said, Behold, the people is one, and they have all one language; and this they begin to do: and now nothing will be restrained from them, which they have imagined to do." **Genesis 11:6**

Simply defined, imagination is the ability to form a mental picture of the actual future. Imagination is our ability to see the future, either through the revelation of the scripture or through the eyes of a mental picture.

"What you do not see, you can not possess."

It is our ability to follow God's plan and pattern for our lives. For unless we build up a mental image in our minds, we will never be able to possess the desired future.

Chapter 1 - What is the Power of Imagination?

God said to Abram… *"And the Lord said unto Abram, after that Lot was separated from him, Lift up now thine eyes, and look from the place where thou art northward, and southward, and eastward, and westward: For all the land which thou seest, to thee will I give it, and to thy seed forever."* **(Genesis13:14-15)**

You can only possess what you can see.

Our mind is the greatest weapon on earth. Inside our mind is the unique ability to form a mental picture through the revelation of the scriptures. Imagination has power to birth vision, purpose, and a future. If you can see it, you can pursue it.

"And the Lord said, Behold, the people is one, and they have all one language; and this they begin to do: and now nothing will be restrained from them, which they have imagined to do." **Genesis11:6**

"Finally, brethren, whatsoever things are true, whatsoever things are honest, whatsoever things are just, whatsoever things are pure, whatsoever things are lovely, whatsoever things are of good report; if there be any virtue, and if there be any praise, think on these things." **Phil4:8**

In my opinion imagination is the most powerful force of the mind. Imagination is not mere fantasy, or evil thoughts from the devil. Although that is also possible. In my own understanding any positive thought that comes from God, is what we are talking about.

"For my thoughts are not your thoughts, neither are your ways my ways, saith the Lord. For as the heavens are higher than the earth, so are my ways higher than your ways, and my thoughts than your thoughts." **Isaiah55:8-9**

Whatsoever thought we allow in our heart, has power to persuade our life.

Imagination has power to transform the life of anyone who truly can take advantage of it.

Chapter 1 - What is the Power of Imagination?

The power of imagination is rewarding because it brings in prosperity and rest. A great man of God once said, make your brain work, it will sweat. Imagination is the power behind wealth creation, technology innovation in science and medicine. Imaginative thoughts are vibration, manifestations of positive energy. The power of imagination is derived through the inspiration of the Holy Spirit.

"Let this mind be in you, which was also in Christ Jesus: Who, being in the form of God, thought it not robbery to be equal with God:" **Phil2:5-6**.

"For who hath known the mind of the Lord, that he may instruct him? but we have the mind of Christ." **1cor2:16**.

Set realistic goals in your life.

It is written, *"And be not conformed to this world: but be ye transformed by the renewing of your mind, that ye may prove what is that good, and acceptable, and perfect, will of God."* **Romans12:2**

Although most unbelievers do impact the world through their inventions, and innovative ideas, but for the most part most unbelievers,are limited to the inspired ideas of the Holy Ghost. It is evil to set goals that are unrealistic and demonic. We must always set goals that are attainable, and realistic in life. You may not be good in everything, but there is something you can do better in life.

What are you good at?

It is vital to develop a realistic approach to your life. It is the power of imagination that will inspire you to see a future in your own inner ability.

Zig Ziglar once said, *"Just about any dummy can succeed, if they chose to"* Every one of us have a purpose and a dream in life."

Although it can manifest differently with other people. In some people, *the power of imagination is positively developed, while in others, it is negatively and wickedly developed.*

Chapter 1 - What is the Power of Imagination?

The power of Imagination makes it possible for those of us in Christ, to boldly say, *"I am in the world but I am not of the world. I live in heavenly places, far above principalities and power."* It gives us the edge to succeed in the midst of challenges and obstacles in life.

"And he said unto them, Ye are from beneath; I am from above: ye are of this world; I am not of this world." **John8:23**

"Ye are of God, little children, and have overcome them: because greater is he that is in you, than he that is in the world." **1John4:4**

"And hath raised us up together, and made us sit together in heavenly places in Christ Jesus:" **Ephesians2:6**

In our imagination, we can travel anywhere; even into space without any obstacles. It can make you feel free, or bound depending how we yield to it.

It is written, *"Know ye not, that to whom ye yield yourselves servants to obey, his servants ye are to whom ye obey; whether of sin unto death, or of obedience unto righteousness?"* **Romans6:16**.

It is written, *"For who hath known the mind of the Lord, that he may instruct him? but we have the mind of Christ."* **1cor2:16**

"Let this mind be in you, which was also in Christ Jesus:" **Phil2:5**

"Keep thy heart with all diligence; for out of it are the issues of life." **Proverb 4:23**

"And be renewed in the spirit of your mind;" **Ephesians4:23**

How do I imagine my future?

Our mind can be transformed and turned around.it has the ability to turn any positive or negative imagination into reality. For us to imagine our future we must first:

Chapter 1 - What is the Power of Imagination?

1. Draw a mental image of a successful future.

Mental pictures are the blueprint for success in life. Mental pictures give us clarity and precision. It defines and narrows our vision in life. More also it makes it easy for us to pursue a particular vision.

It is written, *"Brethren, I count not myself to have apprehended: but this one thing I do, forgetting those things which are behind, and reaching forth unto those things which are before,"* Phil3:13.

The Psalmist said, *"One thing have I desired of the Lord, that will I seek after; that I may dwell in the house of the Lord all the days of my life, to behold the beauty of the Lord, and to enquire in his temple."* **Psalms27:4**

2. Imagination gives birth to purpose

For anyone of us to aspire to accomplish great things in life, we must be driven with a purpose. Imagination gives us that leverage to be driven with a purpose.

3. Associate your life with life coaches and mentor

Mentors are the shortcut to all outstanding careers and vocation in life. If anyone of us must succeed in life, we must have mentors to follow their footsteps.

It is written, *"That ye be not slothful, but followers of them who through faith and patience inherit the promises."* **Hebrews 6:12**

What are we saying?

Whatever God is calling us to do, we must look for people who have done it in time past.

It is written, *"The thing that hath been, it is that which shall be; and that which is done is that which shall be done: and there is no new thing under the sun."* **Ecl1:9**

What we are saying is for everyone to live for a purpose. We must therefore develop purpose, a goal, and a vision for your life and family. Always believe God that there is a way up, a way forward and a way out of any prevailing predicament we find our self. No one know your financial situation better than you.

"It is written Whatsoever thy hand findeth to do, do it with thy might; for there is no work, nor device, nor knowledge, nor wisdom, in the grave, whither thou goest." **Eccl9:10**

Chapter 1 - What is the Power of Imagination?

"For even when we were with you, this we commanded you, that if any would not work, neither should he eat." **2theo3:10**

"The sluggard will not plow by reason of the cold; therefore shall he beg in harvest, and have nothing." **Proverb20:4**

"He also that is slothful in his work is brother to him that is a great waster." **Proverb18:9**

"The soul of the sluggard desireth, and hath nothing: but the soul of the diligent shall be made fat." **Proverb13:4**

"He becometh poor that dealeth with a slack hand: but the hand of the diligent maketh rich." **Proverb10:4**

BENEFITS OF IMAGINATION

1. Imagination inspires us.

If you can dream it God will make it happen for you. If you can dream it, and believe it. There is no demon anywhere in the world that will stop you.

The bible said *"..... and this they begin to do: and now nothing will be restrained from them, which they have imagined to do."* **Genesis11:6**

Imagination is the energy that fuels any great dream in life. If you can be passionate enough to pursue your dream, God will make it happen in your life time.

2. Imagination creates a great future.

Most people that succeed in life are people who are relentless, consistent and committed in their desire to attain the desired goal. If anyone of us must succeed in life, we must learn to be committed, dedicated, disciplined, and focus on whatsoever God has called us to do in life.

Chapter 1 - What is the Power of Imagination?

No man succeeds by luck. Do you want a great future? You must take responsibility right now. For I quote *"Winners do not quit, and those who quit never win in life."*

We are controlled by our most dominant thought. Whatsoever you imagine is what you will witness in your life. God is favorable to us all. He is not a partial God.

"For there is no respect of persons with God." **Romans2:11.**

God will do whatever you ask and seek for him to do for you. He is not a partial God.

"Then Peter opened his mouth, and said, Of a truth I perceive that God is no respecter of persons:" **Acts10:34**

3. Imagination enhances creativity and innovation.

Some of the most influential men on earth today, are men of innovation. It was Steve Job's imaginative ability that gave us the edge we have today on smart phones. For unless you see it, you cannot have it.

CHAPTER 2
The Power of Vision

"Where there is no vision, the people perish: but he that keepeth the law, happy is he" **Proverb29:18.**

The power of vision is our ability to live for purpose, with a dreams, and a desire to pursue and fulfilled it in life. *What do you see that others do not see? What do you hear that others do not hear? God talk to our heart. Is the Holy Spirit talking to you.?*

Often, every time we mention the word Vision, we tend to draw attention to our busy dreams or perhaps what a seer or a prophet said about us.

In my opinion *"vision"* means our ability to see ahead through the power of God-in a dream, or through an audible voice, a revelation, or in a trance. *For unless you imagine a great future for your life, you will not be able to fulfil it.*

God's vision can be communicated to us either through a dream or trance, or as a supernatural apparition. For any vision to make an impact, the visionary must be goal oriented and success driven. The term vision has numerous definitions, depending upon one's perspective.

For most church people, the term vision is often misinterpreted. So many of us claim we have a genuine vision from the Lord. For, unless we are committed, dedicated to working towards the actualization of that vision, it will remain unfulfilled in our lifetime.

It is written *"Verily, verily, I say unto you, Except a corn of wheat fall into the ground and die, it abideth alone: but if it die, it bringeth forth much fruit."* **John12:24**.

For unless we are ready to pay the price for any vision, we will never make an impact with such vision. Every vision from God start small to grow big. Unless you are driven with a purpose, you will be employed to fulfil someone's vision in life.

Chapter 2 - The Power of Vision

It is written, *"For I would that all men were even as I myself. But every man hath his proper gift of God, one after this manner, and another after that."* **1cor7:7**.

Our stardom will only shine whenever we genuinely discover and pursue Divine Vision. Most of us crash in life, because we pursue the vision of our friends and mentors in life. But until we face our own future with love, compassion, and gratitude, we will never make an impact in our life time.

Every one of us have a divine calling from the Lord. It is written, *"For many are called, but few are chosen."* **Mathew22:14**.

The Holy Scripture gave us strict guidelines to follow in other to fulfil our heavenly calling.

It is written *"Wherefore the rather, brethren, give diligence to make your calling and election sure: for if ye do these things, ye shall never fall:"* **2Peter1:10**

Our heavenly vision is unique. We must therefore discover our talent on time and pursue it with every passion in us. For unless we discover it for our lives, we will struggle and be opposed with challenges in life.

"Who hath saved us, and called us with an holy calling, not according to our works, but according to his own purpose and grace, which was given us in Christ Jesus before the world began." **2tim1:9**

Without doubt God had distributed spiritual gift to everyone. Jeremiah said *"Before I formed thee in the belly I knew thee; and before thou camest forth out of the womb I sanctified thee, and I ordained thee a prophet unto the nations."* **Jeremiah1:5**

Apostle Paul said, *"But when it pleased God, who separated me from my mother's womb, and called me by his grace."* **Gal1:15**

Chapter 2 - The Power of Vision

There is no doubt in my heart. I know you are called by God. There is a heavenly assignment concerning your life here on earth. But have you discovered it? Or you are still wonder what to do about your future.

"For I would that all men were even as I myself. But every man hath his proper gift of God, one after this manner, and another after that." **1cor7:7**

"But as God hath distributed to every man, as the Lord hath called every one, so let him walk. And so ordain I in all churches." **1cor7:17**

"Let every man abide in the same calling wherein he was called." **1cor7:20**

"Brethren, let every man, wherein he is called, therein abide with God." **1cor7:24**

It is written *"And he said, Hear now my words: If there be a prophet among you, I the Lord will make myself known unto him in a vision, and will speak unto him in a dream."* **Number12:6**

As believers every one of us must develop a vivid mental image of our future. *"If you can see ahead, know ahead, you will go ahead in life."* Often most of us go to school to pursue a career chosen by our father, or older brother.

For unless we make an early choice in life we will end up in confusion. Vision therefore helps us to make a choice and stick to our choice in life.

Although Vision is essential for organizations and companies. It is recommended that we develop our personal vision in life. However, God's vision must be dynamic and not static. No one just wakes up early in the morning and says, God gave me a vision to become a preacher this morning.

For any vision to speak, there must be a clear calling from God. Secondly there must be a purpose and a burning desire to fulfil such vision from the Lord. We must train ourselves diligently in order to fulfil such a vision from the Lord.

Chapter 2 - The Power of Vision

The significance of a vision from God

Vision enhances focus and promotes unity

Often some of us wander in confusion life. I know of a family member who literally did almost every profession you can think about in life. If I am permitted to say it this way. *"Where there is no vision, the people end up in confusion in life."* Every time you have a genuine vision from God it helps us to be focused in life.

Jesus said, *"For where two or three are gathered together in my name, there am I in the midst of them."* **Mathew 18:20**.

I recommend that we develop a genuine vision from the Lord. May you never end up Jack of all trades, master of none.

God's Vision makes us responsible in life

Men of vision are responsible men of impact in life. Visionaries are men and women who transform the world. Innovators like Mike Zuckerberg, Bill gates will forever be remembered for generation to come.

God's Vision Provides Purpose

Often some of us have no purpose in life. Every time you genuinely have a vision from God, it gives you purpose for living.

God's vision brings out the leadership quality inside of us

As a visionary your leadership skill will be tried. Most church founders start a church and five to ten years later, the church closes. Not because they could not pray correctly. But because they lacked the leadership structure and skill to move the ministry into the next level.

Hindrances to a divine vision from the Lord

-------------------Doubt-------------------

It is written, *"A double minded man is unstable in all his ways."* **James 1:8.** For the most part, everyone around you will try to hinder you against your God-given vision. I like to encourage you. Never doubt the vision you received from the Lord.

Chapter 2 - The Power of Vision

Our heart desire is God's plan and pattern for our life. It is written *"A double minded man is unstable in all his ways."* **James1:8**

------------------ **Unbelief**------------------

Unbelief will destroy any genuine vision from the Lord. Unless you have not heard from the Lord, there is no reason to doubt what God has spoken to you.

Talking about Jesus the bible says, *"And he could there do no mighty work, save that he laid his hands upon a few sick folk, and healed them. And he marvelled because of their unbelief. And he went round about the villages, teaching."* **Mark6:5-6**.

------------------**Fear**------------------

If God has shown you the vision, there is nothing to be afraid of. The least that will happen is that you will fail at your first trial, but as long as you do not quit you will eventually succeed.

Fear of the unknown will make most people not to pursue their heavenly vision in life.

"Thou therefore gird up thy loins, and arise, and speak unto them all that I command thee: be not dismayed at their faces, lest I confound thee before them." **Jer1:17**

Apostle Paul said, *"For a great door and effectual is opened unto me, and there are many adversaries."* **1cor16:9**

-------------------Sin------------------

David made these outstanding remarks, *"Wash me throughly from mine iniquity, and cleanse me from my sin. For I acknowledge my transgressions: and my sin is ever before me. Against thee, thee only, have I sinned, and done this evil in thy sight: that thou mightest be justified when thou speakest, and be clear when thou judgest. Behold, I was shapen in iniquity; and in sin did my mother conceive me."* **Psalms51:2-5**

Chapter 2 - The Power of Vision

Talent will take anyone to the top of their lives, but it will take character to sustain them. Think of a few celebrity that have crashed down to zero the last few years. Every child of the Most High-God must not play around in sin. Sin should never dominate our lives as believers. **(See Romans6:14)**

It is written, *"Ye adulterers and adulteresses, know ye not that the friendship of the world is enmity with God? Whosoever therefore will be a friend of the world is the enemy of God."* **James4:4**

WE MUST REPENT OF OUR SINS

Wherefore seeing we also are compassed about with so great a cloud of witnesses, let us lay aside every weight, and the sin which doth so easily beset us, and let us run with patience the race that is set before us. **Hebrew12:1**.

We must not allow sin to destroy our calling and destiny in life. We must therefore repent of any known sin in our lives before God can restore our destiny.

"For sin shall not have dominion over you: for ye are not under the law, but under grace." **Romans6:14**

Every time we yield to sin, we place ourselves in captivity. We must all strive to forsake sin and do away with every evil that dent our Christian dignity.

Know ye not, that to whom ye yield yourselves servants to obey, his servants ye are to whom ye obey; whether of sin unto death, or of obedience unto righteousness? **Romans6:16**

It is written, *"Be not overcome of evil, but overcome evil with good."* **Romans12:21**.

We must all repent of any know sin that dents our Christian walk with the Lord Jesus Christ.

Apostle Paul had this to say….

Chapter 2 - The Power of Vision

"I find then a law, that, when I would do good, evil is present with me. For I delight in the law of God after the inward man: But I see another law in my members, warring against the law of my mind, and bringing me into captivity to the law of sin which is in my members. O wretched man that I am! who shall deliver me from the body of this death? I thank God through Jesus Christ our Lord. So then with the mind I myself serve the law of God; but with the flesh the law of sin." **Romans7:21-25**

This scripture makes a lot of sense if you examine your own life. Evil is present every time we strive to do good. What shall we say then? Shall we continue in sin, that grace may abound? God forbid. How shall we, that are dead to sin, live any longer therein? **Romans6:1-2**

"Examine yourselves, whether ye be in the faith; prove your own selves. Know ye not your own selves, how that Jesus Christ is in you, except ye be reprobates?" **2cor13:5**

Although most faith people live in denial about the work of the flesh, from my own scriptural understanding everyone operating within the scope of ***Galatians 5:20-21*** is classified as a sinner.

How do I come out of sin?

Repent and confess the Lord Jesus as your Lord. Genuinely stop all evil and unrighteous lifestyle. God will hear your prayers and have mercy.

We must make up our mind for good if we must come out of sin. We must confess, and forsake it in the mighty name of Jesus.

The word says as many as received him, to them gave He power to become the sons of God. Even to them that believe on his name.

Chapter 2 - The Power of Vision

To qualify for divine visitation do the following sincerely;

1) Acknowledge that you are a sinner and that He died for you. **Rom3:23**.

2) Repent of your sins. **Acts 3:19, Luke13:5, 2Peter3:9**

3) Believe in your heart that Jesus died for your sin. **Romans10:10**

4) Confess Jesus as the Lord over your life. **Romans10:10, Acts2:21**

Now repeat this Prayer after me

Say Lord Jesus, I accept you today, as my Lord and my savior, forgive me of my sins wash me with your blood. Right now, I believe, I am sanctified, I am save, I am free, I am free from the Power of sin to serve the Lord Jesus. Thank you Lord for saving me. Amen.

CONCLUSION

"Therefore my people are gone into captivity, because they have no knowledge: and their honourable men are famished, and their multitude dried up with thirst.." **Isaiah5:13**

There is power in imagination. Where do you see your life five to ten years from now? If you no idea of where your life is going, you will eventually go nowhere.

God said to Abraham as far as your eyes can see, I will give it to you. Remember we are the seed of Abraham.

It is written, *"They answered and said unto him, Abraham is our father. Jesus saith unto them, If ye were Abraham's children, ye would do the works of Abraham."* **John8:39**

Are you still struggling with any addiction or stress related illness in life. It is time to set the record straight. For unless you repent, God is not committed to restore your life.

Chapter 2 - The Power of Vision

In my opinion repentance is the key to deliverance in life. Everyone that desired testimonies in life, must repent of their sins. Effective prayer begins by faith confession, repentance for salvation to be effective.

"Therefore if any man be in Christ, he is a new creature: old things are passed away; behold, all things are become new." **2cor5:17**

What must I do to determine my divine visitation?

To determine divine visitation you must be born again. The word says as many as received him, to them gave He power to become the sons of God. Even to them that believe on his name.

To qualify for divine visitation do the following sincerely;

1) Acknowledge that you are a sinner and that He died for you. **Rom3:23**.

2) Repent of your sins. **Acts 3:19, Luke13:5, 2Peter3:9**

3) Believe in your heart that Jesus died for your sin. **Romans10:10**

4) Confess Jesus as the Lord over your life. **Romans10:10, Acts2:21**

Chapter 2 - The Power of Vision

Now repeat this Prayer after me

Say Lord Jesus, I accept you today, as my Lord and my savior, forgive me of my sins wash me with your blood. Right now, I believe, I am sanctified, I am save, I am free, I am free from the Power of sin to serve the Lord Jesus. Thank you Lord for saving me. Amen.

Congratulations: YOU ARE NOW A BORN AGAIN CHRISTAIN

I adjure you to watch the Spirit of God bear witness with your Spirit confirming His word with signs following. The word says The Spirit itself beareth witness with our spirit, that we are the children of God. Join a bible believing church or join us on our weekly and Sunday worship services at 343 Sanford Avenue Newark New Jersey 07106.

WISDOM KEYS

Every Productive Society is a society heading to the top

Millions of Nigerians run away from Nigeria, very few Nigerians stay in Nigeria.

My decision to return Nigeria is the will of God for my life

My short coming in America after 18 years, trained me to be wise, to think, reflect and reason appropriately.

If you train your mind to reason it will train your hands to earn money.

It is absurd to use the money of the heathen to build the kingdom of the living God.

Every Ministry reveals its agenda and goal either at the beginning or at the end. Be careful of your life it is your first Ministry.

The average American mind is conditioned for a continual quest to get new things and (discard the former) and throw away old things.

Chapter 2 - The Power of Vision

When I considered well, my BMW jeep became my initial deposit for the work of the ministry in Nigeria

Everyone is waiting for you to change your mind until you change your thinking nothing changes around you.

Multiple academic degrees in other discipline gave me the chance to think, reflect and reason

What so everyone are thinking and reflecting at the moment reveals you to the time and the now factor

All events and intents are the product of precise thought processes, accurate reason every event is designed for a designated timeline

Wisdom is your ability to think, to create and invent. If you can think wise enough you will come out of penury

The distance between you and success is your creative ability to think reason and reflect accurate.

Success is the result of hard work, commitment resolve and determination learning from past mistakes and failing.

If you organize your mind you have organized your life and destiny.

There is a thin line between success and failure. If you look above and beyond you are on your way to success.

Wealth is your ability to think, power is your ability to reason and success is your ability to be informed.

If you can make use of your mind by thinking and reasoning God will make use of your life and destiny.

Think and Be Great

Reflect, Reason, think and be great

Famous people are born of woman

Chapter 2 - The Power of Vision

That you will make it is your intention; that you will survive is your resolve, that you will succeed with changes is your determination, personal efforts and hard work.

No man was born a failure. Lack of vision is the end product of failure.

Working with mental patients encourages and aspire me to be a productive observant and dedicated to my assignment.

Successful people are not magicians, it is the will power combined with hard work, and determination and a resolve to succeed that make them succeed.

In the unequivocal state of the mind, intention is not a location or a position it is the state of the mind.

So many people think that they think. The mind is used to think reflect and reason. You will remain blind with your eye open until you can see with your mind by thinking.

There is no favoritism in accurate and precise calculation

Although knowledge is power, information is the key and gateway to a great future.

It will take the hand of God to move the hand of man.

With the backing of the great wise God, nothing will disconnect you from your inheritance.

As long as you have wisdom and understanding of God, Satan and evil cannot manipulate your life and destiny.

You have come this far by yourself judgment and decision you have made in the past, now lean and listen to God for another dimension of greatness.

Great people are common people it is extra ordinary effort and the price of sacrifice that produces greatness.

As a mental direct care worker I saw a great pastor and a motivational speaker within myself.

Menial job does not reduce your self-worth, until you resolve to achieve greatness see greatness in all you do; you will never count in your community

Chapter 2 - The Power of Vision

The principle of Jesus will solve your gambling and addiction problems

The man of Jesus will lead you into heaven,

Everyone have their self-appraisal and what they think about you. Until you discover yourself other opinion about you will alter the real you.

Supervisors and directors are just a position in the chain of command in a work place. Never allow your supervisor hierarchy to alter your opinion about yourself.

Everyone can come out of debt if they make up their mind.

That I am not a decision maker at work does not diminish my contribution to my world.

Although it appears like it was a poor decision to accept a direct care employment at a psychiatric hospital as I reflect of my nine years of experience, it became apparent that I have learnt and experienced enough for my next assignment.

Self-encouragement and determination is a resolve of the heart.

The Power of Imagination by Franklin N. Abazie

If you are determined to make a difference, and do the things that make a difference you will eventually make a difference.

Good things do not come easy

Short cuts will cut your life short.

Those who look ahead move ahead.

Life is all about making an impact. In your life time strive to make an impact in your community.

Make friends and connect with people who are moving ahead of you in life.

If you can look around well you have come a long way in your life, made a lot of difference and realized a lot of success in life.

If you are my old friend, hurry up to reach out to me before I become a stranger to you.

Everything I am blessed with inspirations from God, that change my definition and interpretation of the world around me.

I thought I was stagnant and lonely until I looked around and noticed my children running around and my wife cooking.

Chapter 2 - The Power of Vision

At 40 I resigned my Job to seek the Lord forever.

My ministry took a drastic rise to the top when the wisdom of God visited me with knowledge and understanding.

You will be a better person if you understand the characteristics of your personality – your mood swings attitudes and habits.

It is the seed of love you sow into the heart of a child and a woman that you reap in due time.

Love is not selfish, love share everything including the concealed secrets of the mind.

As long as you have a prayer life and a bible; you will never feel lonely, rejected and idle in the race of life.

When good friends disconnect from you, let them go, they might have seen something new in a different direction.

Confidence in yourself and in God is the only way to bring you out of captivity

Never train a child to waste his/her time.

The mind is the greatest assets of a great future.

The Power of Imagination by Franklin N. Abazie

You walk by common sense run by principles and fly by instruction.

Those who fly in flight of life fly alone.

Up in the air you are alone. No one can toll you accept the compass of knowledge and information

I have seen a tolling vehicle I have seen a tolling ship I have never seen a tolling airplane.

I exercise my judgment and make a decision every minute of the day.

Decisions are crucial, critical and vital with reference to your future.

So many people wish for a great future. You can only work towards a great future.

Your celebrity status began when you discovered your talent. What are you good at? Work at it with all commitment.

Prayers will sustain you but the wisdom of God will prosper you.

When I met Oyedepo, his teachings changed my perspective, but when I met Ibiyeomie; His teaching changed my perception.

I will be successful in ministry if only I concentrate and focus my energy in the work of the ministry.

It took the late Dr. Vincent Pearle Norman's book to open my mind towards kingdom success.

CHAPTER 3

PRAYER OF SALVATION

"Neither is there salvation in any other: for there is none other name under heaven given among men, whereby we must be saved." **Acts4:12.**

What must I do to determine my salvation?

To be saved we must be born again! The word says as many as received him, to them gave He power to become the sons of God. Even to them that believe on his name.

To qualify for divine visitation do the following sincerely,

1) Acknowledge that you are a sinner and that He died for you. **Rom3:23.**

2) Repent of your sins. **Acts 3:19, Luke13:5, 2Peter3:9**

3) Believe in your heart that Jesus died for your sin. **Romans10:10**

4) Confess Jesus as the Lord over your life. **Romans10:10, Acts2:21**

Now repeat this Prayer after me

Say Lord Jesus, I accept you today, as my Lord and my savior, forgive me of my sins wash me with your blood. Right now, I believe, I am sanctified, I am save, I am free, I am free from the Power of sin to serve the Lord Jesus. Thank you Lord for saving me. Amen.

Chapter 3 - Prayer of Salvation

MIRACLE CARE OUTREACH

"...But that the members should have the same care one for another" **1cor12:25**

We are all members of the body of Christ. Jesus commanded us to love our neighbor as ourselves. This includes caring for one another as a member of one body. True love is expressed in caring and giving. The word says for God so Love He gave….

Reach out to someone in need of Jesus, help someone in crisis find Christ. Look out and prove your love to Jesus by caring and inviting your friends and associates to find Jesus the Healer.

Invite your friends to our Home Care Cell Fellowship (Miracle chapel Intl Satellite fellowship) In the USA at 33 Schley Street Newark New Jersey 07112.

If you are in Nigeria—**MIRACLE OF GOD MINISTRIES**

A.K.A"MIRACLE CHAPEL INTL"
Mpama –Egbu-Owerri Imo state Nigeria.

(Home Care Cell fellowship Group). We meet every Tuesday at 6:00pm-7:00pm.

LIFE IS NOT ALL ABOUT DURATION BUT ITS ALL ABOUT DONATION

What does the above statement mean?....

"Life consists not in accumulation of material wealth.." **Luke12:15.**

"But it's all about liberality....meaning-what you can give and share with others." **Proverb11:25.**

When you live for others--You live forever- because you out live your generation by the legacy you live behind after you depart into glory to be with the Lord. But when you live to yourself - you are reduced to self—you are easily forgotten when you die and depart in glory.

Permit me to admonish you today to live your life to be a blessing to a soul connected to you today.

Chapter 3 - Prayer of Salvation

I want you to know that so many souls are connected and looking up to you, and through you so many souls will be saved and rescued from destruction. Will you disciple someone today to find Jesus Christ?

"As a genuine Christian; it is your duty to evangelize Jesus Christ to all you meet on your way. Jesus is still in the healing business-Jesus is still doing miracles from time of old to now.

Therefore tell someone about Jesus Christ today, disciple and bring them to Church."

John 1:45 Philip findeth Nathanael....

Please to prove the sincerity of your love for God today; please become a soul winner. The dignity of your Christianity is hidden in your boldness to proclaim and evangelize Jesus Christ to all you meet on your way.

There is a question mark on the integrity of your Christianity until you become a life soul winner. Invite someone to join us worship the Lord Jesus this coming Sunday.

MIRACLE OF GOD MINISTRIES

PILLARS OF THE COMMISSION

We Believe Preach and Practice the following,

1) We believe and preach Salvation to every living human being

2) We believe and preach Repentance and forgiveness of sins

3) We believe and preach the baptism of the Holy Spirit and Spiritual gifts

4) We believe and teach the Prosperity

5) We believe and preach Divine Healing and Miracles (Signs &Wonder)

6) We believe and preach Faith

7) We believe and Proclaim the Power of God (Supernatural)

8) We believe and Proclaim Praise& Worship to God

9) We believe and preach Wisdom

10) We believe and preach Holiness (Consecration)

11) We believe and preach Vision

12) We believe and teach the Word of God

13) We believe and teach Success

14) We believe and practice Prayer

15) We believe and teach Deliverance

This 15 stones form the Pillars of Our Commission.

Become part of this church family and follow this great move of God.

MY HEART FELT PRAYER FOR YOU

It is my prayer that you testify today about the goodness of the Lord. I desire for you to have an encounter with our Lord Jesus Christ.

Now let me Pray for you:

Lord Jesus give this precious one reading this material heavenly vision that will give them purpose to live the remaining days of their lives. Lord God of heaven open a new chapter in the life of this precious love one reading this book today. May all their prayers be answered in the mighty name of Jesus. We thank you Jesus for hearing us. In Jesus mighty name. Amen.

CHAPTER 4
ABOUT THE AUTHOR

Rev Franklin N Abazie is the founding and Presiding Pastor of Miracle of God Ministries with headquarters in Newark, New Jersey USA and a branch church in Owerri- Imo State Nigeria. He is following the footsteps of one of his mentors, Oral Roberts (Healing Evangelist) of the blessed memory.

The Lord passed Oral Roberts healing mantle two days before he went to be with the Lord at age 91 into the hand of healing evangelist-Rev Franklin N Abazie in a vision.

In all his services the Power and Presence of God is present to heal all in his audience. He is an ordained man of God with a Healing Ministry reviving the healing and miracle ministry of Jesus Christ of Nazareth.

Pastor Franklin N Abazie, is called by God with a unique mandate:

"THE MOMENT IS DUE TO IMPACT YOUR WORLD THROUGH THE REVIVAL OF THE HEALING & MIRACLE MINISTRY OF JESUS CHRIST OF NAZARETH.
I AM SENDING YOU TO RESTORE HEALTH UNTO THEE AND I WILL HEAL THEE OF THY WOUNDS. SAID THE LORD OF HOST"

He is a gifted ardent Teacher of the word of God who operates also in the office of a Prophet, generating and attracting undeniable signs & wonders, special miracles and healings, with apostolic fireworks of the Holy Ghost.

He is the founding and presiding senior Pastor of this fast growing Healing ministry.

Chapter 4 - About the Author

He has written over 86 inspirational, healing and transforming books covering almost all aspect of divine healing and life. He is happily married and blessed with children.

BOOKS BY REV FRANKLIN N ABAZIE

1) Commanding Abundance
2) The outcome of faith
3) Understanding the secret of prevailing prayers
4) Understanding the secret of the man God uses
5) Activating my due Season
6) Overcoming Divine Verdicts
7) The Outcome of Divine Wisdom
8) Understanding God's Restoration Mandate
9) Walking in the Victory and Authority of the truth
10) Gods Covenant Exemption
11) Destiny Restoration Pillars
12) Provoking Acceptable Praise
13) Understanding Divine Judgment
14) Activating Angelic Re-enforcement
15) Provoking Un-Merited Favor
16) The Benefits of the Speaking faith
17) Understanding Divine Arrangement

18) Understanding Divine Healing
19) The Mystery of Endurance
20) Obeying Divine Instructions
21) Understanding the Voice of God
22) Never give up on Hope
23) The prevailing Power of faith
24) Understanding Divine Prosperity
25) The Reward of Prayer
26) Covenant Keys to Answered Prayers
27) Activating the Forces of Vengeance
28) Put your faith to work
29) Where is your trust?
30) The Audacity of the Blood of Jesus
31) Redeeming Your Days
32) The force of Vision
33) Breaking the shackles of Family Curses
34) Wisdom for Marriage Stability
35) The winners Faith
36) The Prayer solution
37) The power of Prayer
38) The Effective Strategy of Prayer
39) The prayer that works
40) Walking in Forgiveness
41) The power of the grace of God

42) The power of Persistence
43) Overcoming Divine verdicts
44) The audacity of the blood of Jesus.
45) The prevailing power of the blood of Jesus
46) The benefit of the speaking faith.
47) Fearless faith
48) Redeeming Your Days.
49) The Supernatural Power of Prophecy
50) The companionship of the Holy Spirit
51) Understanding Divine Judgement
52) Understanding Divine Prosperity
53) Dominating Controlling Forces
54) The winners Faith
55) Destiny Restoration Pillars
56) Developing Spiritual Muscles
57) Inexplicable faith
58) The lifestyle of Prayer
59) Developing a positive attitude in life.
60) The mystery of Divine supply
61) Encounter with God's Power
62) Walking in love
63) Praying in the Spirit
64) How to provoke your testimony

65) Walking in the reality of the Anointing
66) The reality of new birth
67) The price of freedom
68) The Supernatural power of faith
69) The Power of Persistence
70) The intellectual components of Redemption
71) Overcoming Fear
72) The Force of Vision
73) Overcoming Prevailing Challenges
74) The Power of the Grace of God
75) My life & Ministry
76) The Mystery of Praise

MIRACLE OF GOD MINISTRIES

NIGERIA CRUSADE 2012

MIRACLE OF GOD MINISTRIES
NIGERIA CRUSADE 2012

MIRACLE OF GOD MINISTRIES

NIGERIA CRUSADE

2012

MIRACLE OF GOD MINISTRIES

NIGERIA CRUSADE

2012

www.ingramcontent.com/pod-product-compliance
Lightning Source LLC
Chambersburg PA
CBHW021444080526
44588CB00009B/683